T0398705

Dear Parent:
Your child's love of reading starts here!

Every child learns to read in a different way and at his or her own speed. Some go back and forth between reading levels and read favorite books again and again. Others read through each level in order. You can help your young reader improve and become more confident by encouraging his or her own interests and abilities. From books your child reads with you to the first books he or she reads alone, there are I Can Read Books for every stage of reading:

SHARED READING
Basic language, word repetition, and whimsical illustrations, ideal for sharing with your emergent reader

BEGINNING READING
Short sentences, familiar words, and simple concepts for children eager to read on their own

READING WITH HELP
Engaging stories, longer sentences, and language play for developing readers

READING ALONE
Complex plots, challenging vocabulary, and high-interest topics for the independent reader

I Can Read Books have introduced children to the joy of reading since 1957. Featuring award-winning authors and illustrators and a fabulous cast of beloved characters, I Can Read Books set the standard for beginning readers.

A lifetime of discovery begins with the magical words **"I Can Read!"**

Visit www.icanread.com for information
on enriching your child's reading experience.

Visit www.zonderkidz.com/icanread for more faith-based
I Can Read! titles from Zonderkidz.

"My Father has given all things to me."
—Luke 10:22

ZONDERKIDZ

Big Bugs, Little Bugs
Copyright © 2011 by Zonderkidz

An **I Can Read Book**

Requests for information should be addressed to:
Zonderkidz, 3900 *Sparks Drive SE, Grand Rapids, Michigan 49546*

Library of Congress Cataloging-in-Publication Data

Big bugs, little bugs.
     p. cm. — (ICR standards. Level 2)
  ISBN 978-0-310-72186-4 (softcover)
   1. Insects—Juvenile literature. 2. Nature—Religious aspects—Christianity—Juvenile
literature.
  QL467.2.B526 2011
  595.7—dc22   2010020337

Editor: *Mary Hassinger*
Art direction & design: *Jody Langley*

Printed in China

21 /DSC/ 10 9 8 7 6

··· MADE·BY·GOD ···

Big Bugs, Little Bugs

CONTENTS

God made it all,

and he made it all good.

He made bees that sting,

ants that crawl,

and the gentle flying …

BUTTERFLIES!

God put butterflies

all over the world.

But not where it is very cold.

Some butterflies fly up to

2,000 miles to find

a warm place to live.

There are about

18,000 kinds of butterflies!

Some kinds are:

Monarch

Tiger swallowtail

Zebra swallowtail

Goliath birdwing

Butterflies live in groups
called flutters.
They live six to eight months
and grow from 1/8-inch wide to
12 inches wide.
Butterflies can fly up to 12
miles an hour!

God blessed butterflies with

colorful wings.

These colors help protect

and hide them from danger.

God made butterflies very colorful,

but he made another bug

that is almost always

black and white …

GOLIATH BEETLES!

The goliath beetle is the
largest beetle in the world.
They are two to four inches long
and weigh three to four
ounces.

The goliath beetle can be
found in tropical parts of Africa.
They use their sharp, strong claws
to climb trees and branches
to find sap and fruit to eat.

The male beetle has a Y-shaped
horn that it uses to
help fight for food it finds
in the trees.

The goliath beetle can fly.

Their strong wings make them

sound like a helicopter!

God made the very large

goliath beetle.

He made a much smaller beetle too.

He made the bright, little …

LIGHTNING BUGS!

Lightning bugs are also
called fireflies.
There are 2,000 kinds of
lightning bugs.
They live from two
months to a year.

Lightning bugs can grow to
be about one inch long—as big
as a paperclip.

Fireflies have special body parts that make them glow. When they glow, the bugs are talking to each other, attracting other bugs, or trying to scare other bugs away.

Adult fireflies are not
the only ones that glow.
In some kinds, the larvae and
eggs might even glow!
Long ago, in China,
people caught fireflies to
make lanterns.

When they are young, fireflies eat
bugs like snails and other
fireflies.
Scientists are not sure what
adult fireflies eat—maybe nothing!

When God made lightning bugs,

he made them glow.

He made another bug that

would rather hide.

It is the …

PRAYING MANTISES!

There are about 1,800
kinds of praying mantises.
They live all over the world
but not where it snows
all the time.

The praying mantis got its
name because of how it looks.
Its long front legs are
bent up and together and look
like someone praying!

28

The praying mantis is almost
always green or brown.
This means it can hide on leaves
or branches.
The head of the praying mantis
can turn almost in a circle!

The color of the praying mantis

and the way it moves

make it easier for

this bug to catch its food of flies,

moths, crickets, and more.

God knew exactly what he
was doing!
Praying mantises help keep
gardens healthy and growing
by catching many pests.

Some bugs are pests.

Some bugs are helpers.

But no matter what we think

of bugs, they are a special creation

from God!